The Holy Spirit and the Greatest Adventure

Gracie Jagla
Illustrated by Ted Schluenderfritz

OSV kids
Huntington, Indiana

Nihil Obstat
Msgr. Michael Heintz, Ph.D.
Censor Librorum
Imprimatur
✠ Kevin C. Rhoades
Bishop of Fort Wayne-South Bend
April 19, 2023

The *Nihil Obstat* and *Imprimatur* are official declarations that a book is free from doctrinal or moral error. It is not implied that those who have granted the *Nihil Obstat* and *Imprimatur* agree with the contents, opinions, or statements expressed.

29 28 27 26 25 24 1 2 3 4 5 6 7 8 9

Our Sunday Visitor Publishing Division
Our Sunday Visitor, Inc.
200 Noll Plaza
Huntington, IN 46750
www.osv.com
1-800-348-2440

ISBN: 978-1-68192-983-5 (Inventory No. T2718)
1. JUVENILE NONFICTION—Religion—Christianity.
2. JUVENILE NONFICTION—Religious—Christian—Inspirational.
3. RELIGION—Christianity—Catholic.

LCCN: 2023946378

Cover and interior design: Lindsey Riesen
Cover and interior art: Ted Schluenderfritz

PRINTED IN TURKEY

In thanksgiving for all those who draw me closer to the Holy Spirit: Lucy, Kathy, and of course our Blessed Mother. — GJ

To Brendan Jones, my pen pal, who loves the Holy Spirit. — TS

Have you ever wondered how God's love is spread?
Or how the Church works, and who guides where it's led?

It's God's Holy Spirit — he's one of the three,
the Persons divine in the bless'd Trinity.

A long time ago, he performed a great sign.
The truth of his message still echoes through time.

It starts with adventure like you've never known,
when heaven touched earth, and God's fire was sown.

A whisper ran through the small upper room
just a few weeks after Christ rose from the tomb.

All huddled around were apostles and friends,
awaiting the promise that Jesus would send.

He'd promised he'd send them his Spirit so great.
But first in the city he told them to wait.

So when would this promise of Jesus come true?
They stayed close and prayed, not sure what to do.

Meanwhile in heaven, a great big delight
was bubbling over — the timing was right!

Today, God's own Spirit would come down to earth —
the day of the Church's own glorious birth!

And who is God's Spirit? He's pure, perfect love!
The love of the Father and Son up above.

Divine, full of power, he comes many ways.
Sometimes, he's like fire! A dove, other days.

When he is with you, he lights you up bright.
Like fireflies, you gleam through the darkness of night.

For so many years, the Holy Spirit did long
to come and fill hearts gone astray and gone wrong.

At last, one great day in a small upper room,
the apostles were gathered in prayer ... and then, BOOM!

The Spirit raced down; nothing stood in his way.
He whirled all around them — today was the day!

His mission was clear: These apostles he'd need
to build up the Church by their prayer and their lead.

They'd need to be brave and stick close by his side,
to spread word of Jesus to souls far and wide.

So he rained down a show'r of fire through the air.
It came down and rested on top of their hair!

A heat spread right through them, from their heads to their toes.
Their hearts grew three sizes and started to glow.

With hearts now aflame and created anew,
they followed him out to tell other folks, too.

But people spoke languages of many kinds —
Now how could God's message reach all of their minds?

The Spirit gave aid, as they knew that he could.
Miraculously, everyone understood!

As townspeople witnessed the joy of this day,
they wanted to join this great Church right away.

Three thousand were baptized. The Church had begun!
But there was more work that would need to be done.

Peter
Andrew
James
John
Philip
Bartholomew
Matthew
Thomas
James the Less
Simon
Jude
Mathias

The earth shook with glee when the Spirit arrived.
The world was alight — it transformed and revived.

Up mountains, 'cross seas, the apostles all went,
just laughing with glory at what heaven sent.

The Spirit led Paul and Saint Peter as well,
hearts blazing, both eager Christ's story to tell.

Even in danger, they smiled so bright.

Their hearts were like lions — all brave and no fright.

He stood by the martyrs, who held their heads high.
His love gave them courage to give up their lives.

And wisdom he breathed in the heart of each pope,
inspiring them with his counsel and hope.

He walked with Teresa down Calcutta's street.

He kissed every baby that John Paul would meet.

He led Juan Diego to Tepeyac's hill,

gave Monica patience and trust in God's will.

He held dear Bakhita when she was oppressed.

With André he stood, and he welcomed each guest.

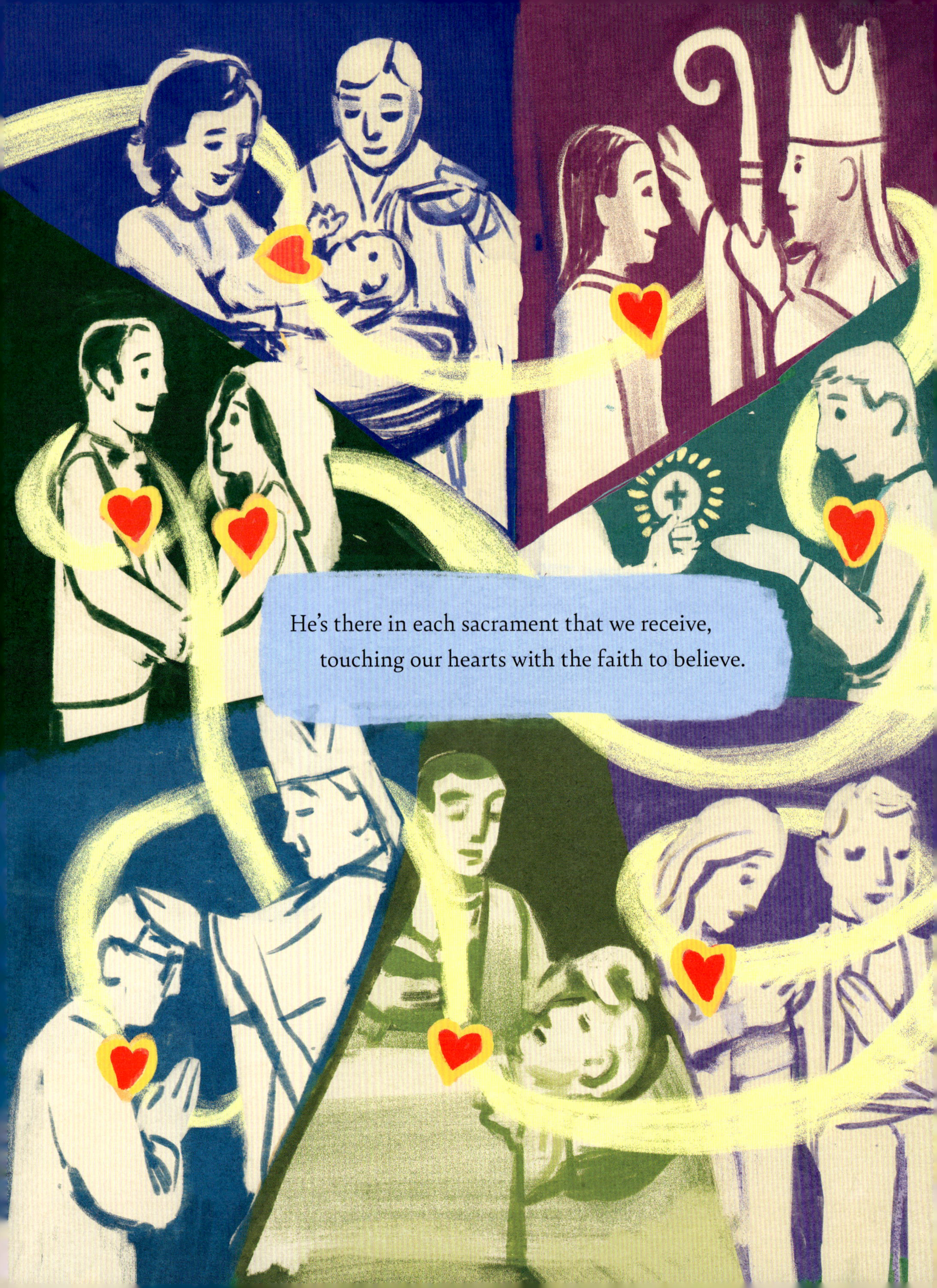

He's there in each sacrament that we receive,
touching our hearts with the faith to believe.

And now in your home, when your family's in prayer,
God's Spirit flies down, and he joins you right there!

The Spirit's still working and blessing today.
He wants you to join him in your special way!

If you want your heart to be caught by this flame,
to live in God's Spirit and praise his great name,

Don't wait one more second! It's easy to do.
Say, "Come, Holy Spirit!" and he'll rush right to you.

More books from Gracie Jagla

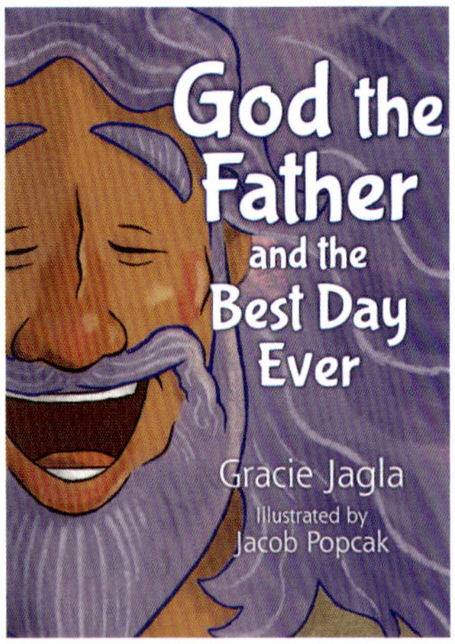

God the Father and the Best Day Ever

With beautiful illustrations and memorable rhyme, this book tells the sweeping story of God's love for us since the beginning of time. Your child will learn how Jesus' life, death, and resurrection opened heaven, so we can spend eternity with God.

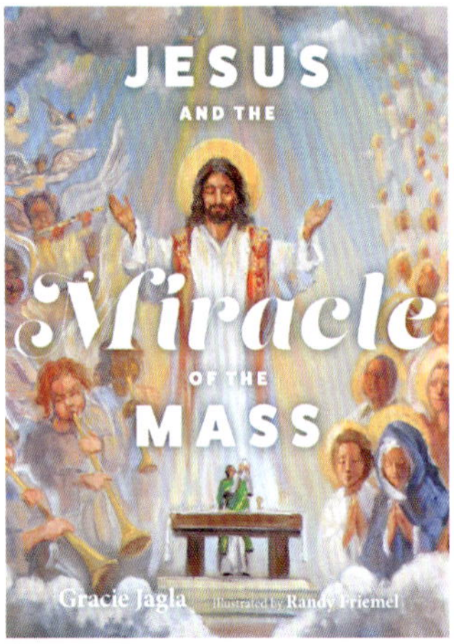

Jesus and the Miracle of the Mass

A miracle occurs at every Mass — the bread and wine on the altar are transformed into the real presence of Jesus. Told from the unique and intimate perspective of Jesus himself, this story explains the incredible gift that the Eucharist is for us.

The Night the Saints Saved Christmas

What happens when Saint Nick awakes on Christmas Eve with a sore throat and itchy nose? Journey with the saints in this adventurous story when they unite to deliver the presents, concluding with a touching reminder about the true meaning of Christmas.

Other books from OSV Kids

In This Catholic Church
by Maura Roan McKeegan

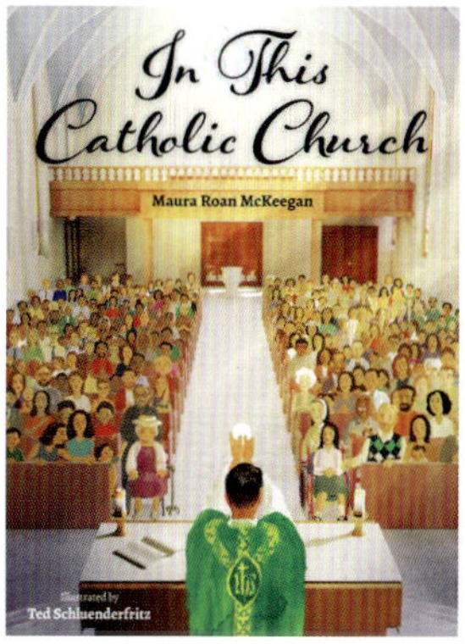

In This Catholic Church, a beautifully illustrated cumulative tale, celebrates our Church as a true family, from the people and families in the pews to the priest at the altar, and the love of Jesus Christ who abides in the hearts of his people.

Arthur the Clumsy Altar Server
by Theresa Kiser

In this endearing children's story filled with charming illustrations, Arthur demonstrates perseverance, humility, and an unquenchable love of the Lord in pursuing his dream. Children will learn from Arthur that what matters most is the sincere desire to serve God — not performing perfectly.

Saintly Rhymes Through the Year
by Meghan Bausch

Five years after perennial favorite ***Saintly Rhymes for Modern Times*** was first published, author and illustrator Meghan Bausch is back with ***Saintly Rhymes Through the Year***. This all-new treasury highlights multiple saints each month with colorful illustrations and catchy rhymes, teaching children that everyone is called to be a saint!

Jesus, Were You Little?
by Sally Metzger

In ***Jesus, Were You Little?*** children full of questions and wonder take readers on a journey of discovery, making Jesus real and relatable to young and old. With innocent curiosity, children ask the King of kings if he ever climbed a tree, spilled his milk, or skinned his knee.

About the Author

Gracie Jagla is blessed to be a wife and mother of three little children. She writes faithful Catholic books infused with a dash of imagination and a sprinkle of grace. Her prayer is that her books bring families closer to Christ and make God smile in the process! Find her award-winning books, including *The Night the Saints Saved Christmas* and *Jesus and the Miracle of the Mass* at graciejagla.com.

About the Illustrator

Ted Schluenderfritz is the illustrator of several books, including The Old and New series, *The Attic Saint*, *Portrait of the Son*, and *In This Catholic Church*. He and his wife, Rachel, just published *The Narrow Gate*, their first book together. They also produce a Catholic website for children: www.5sparrows.com. You can view more of his work on Instagram @schluenderfritz and 5Sparrows.com.